ICDL®/ECDL®

Word Processing

Using Microsoft® Word

Syllabus Version 6.0

Published by: **Conor Jordan**

Arthurstown

New Ross

Co. Wexford

E-mail: conorjordan@gmail.com

Web: www.digidiscover.com

International Computer Driving Licence, ICDL, European Computer Driving Licence, ECDL are all registered Trade Marks of The International Computer Driving Licence Foundation Limited.

Microsoft®, Windows®, Word®, Excel®, PowerPoint®, Access® and Outlook® are trademarks of the Microsoft Corporation. Screenshots and names were used with permission from Microsoft.

Conor Jordan is unaffiliated with Microsoft or The International Computer Driving Licence Foundation Limited.

The intent of this manual is to provide a guide to students and teachers to help them understand the current ICDL syllabus and the features associated with using the application as part of the curriculum.

Conor Jordan does not guarantee students will pass their respective exams as a result of reading this manual. Its purpose is to enable students to gain a greater understanding of the application which may or may not help them achieve their desired results in exams.

Revision sections are for practice purposes only and are not official ICDL tests. Sample tests for each module can be downloaded from the ICDL website to prepare students for their exams.

Aims

The aim of this manual is to give students and teachers a clear understanding of the features and functions of Microsoft Word required for ICDL certification. It aims to achieve this by providing a step-by-step tutorial designed to provide learners with the skills required to use the basic elements of the application.

Objectives

On completion of this manual, learners should be able to:

- Use the basic functions of Microsoft Word
- Create documents
- Format documents
- Create and format objects
- Carry out a mail merge
- Prepare outputs with page setup and printing

Downloading the Work Files

Work files associated with this manual provides the opportunity to practice the techniques outlined without having to type and format many documents saving the learner time to focus on the practical exercises. An internet connection is required to download the files. Visit www.digidiscover.com/downloads and click on the manual you are using.

Files should be saved in an ECDL folder in your Documents folder on your computer.

Contents

Section 1 – Using Microsoft Word

Introduction

Microsoft Word is a useful word processing application with plenty of features allowing the user to create a range of documents.

You can create letters, reports, essays, resumes as well as books, shopping lists and articles.

Users can create templates for web pages with Microsoft Word, translate languages, insert 3D models and proof-read your work

In this tutorial, you will learn how to use the many functions of Microsoft Word that you can use to create a range of documents

Opening Word

1. Click on the **Start** button on the left-hand side of the screen

2. Scroll through the list of applications until you find the **Word** icon
3. Click on the **Word** icon

   The **Home** screen appears

Open a New Document

1. Display the **Home** screen
2. Click on **Blank Document**

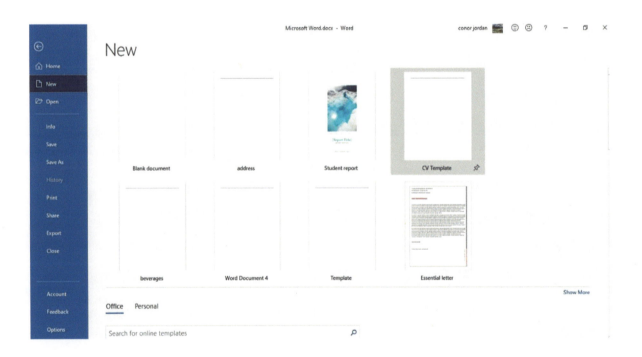

Layout of the Word Screen

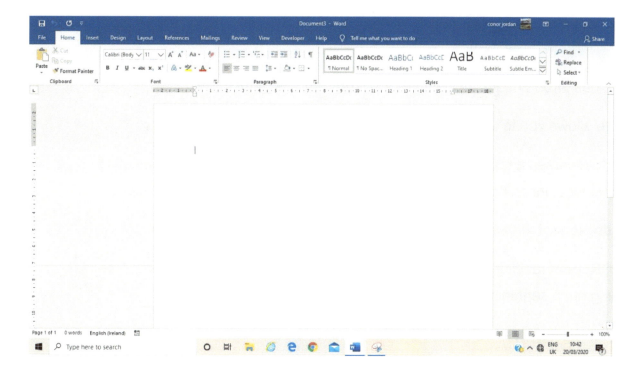

The top line is the **Title Bar** showing the document in use

The **Quick Access Toolbar** has options including **Save, Undo and**

Redo The **File** tab has functions such as **Open, Save, Print** and **Close**

Under this toolbar is the **Ribbon** grouped into **Tabs** containing various

functions Hover over a button to see its name **(ToolTip)**

The **Status Bar** on the bottom of the window displays messages about current

tasks The right of the **Status Bar** contains **Views** buttons and a **Zoom** slider

The **Taskbar** on the bottom of the screen contains buttons for each active task

Quick Access Toolbar

This has three buttons including **Save, Undo** and **Repeat/Redo**

Save allows you to save a copy of your document onto your computer

Undo reverses a task you have carried out in Microsoft Word such as deleting a sentence, inserting a picture or deleting a table

Redo/Repeat allows you to reverse an Undo

The **Repeat** function allows you to automatically perform a task again such as typing out a sentence or copying a picture to a document

To the right of **Repeat/Redo** is the **Customise Quick Access Toolbar**

Here you have options to choose what you want to be included on the **Quick Access Toolbar**

Closing a Word Document

Ensure that you save a document before closing it. Word usually prompts the user before closing a document but it is good practice to develop the habit of saving work regularly.

1. Click on the **File** tab
2. Choose the **Close** option on the left-hand side of the screen

You will be prompted to save the document

3. Choose either **Save** (Save the Document), **Don't Save** (Don't Save the Document) or **Cancel** (To Cancel the Save)

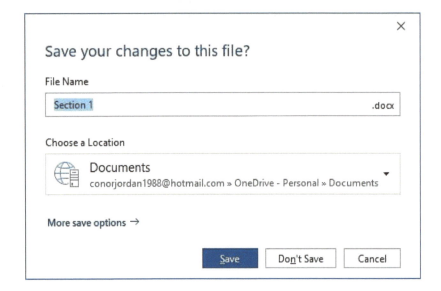

4. Ensure you save your document before closing it

Closing the Word Application

1. Click on the **Close** button on the right of the **Title Bar**

This will close the Word application

Using A Template

1. Display the **Home** screen
2. Click on the **New** option
3. Click on **Personal**

   This will display a range of templates to choose from

Office   Personal

4. Select the **CV Template**

New

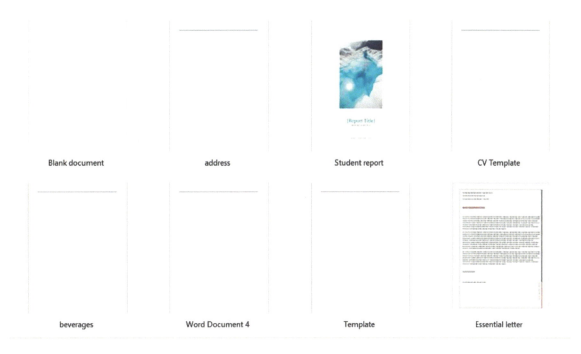

Blank document	address	Student report	CV Template
beverages	Word Document 4	Template	Essential letter

A Curriculum Vitae template is opened

Saving Documents

Use the **Save As** option to save a new document and choose a location for it on your computer (Usually in **Documents**)

Use the **Save** option to update/overwrite a current document

1. Select the **File Tab** on the left of the ribbon
2. Click **Save As**
3. With **Computer** selected, click on the **Browse** button
4. Choose a location on your computer to save your document

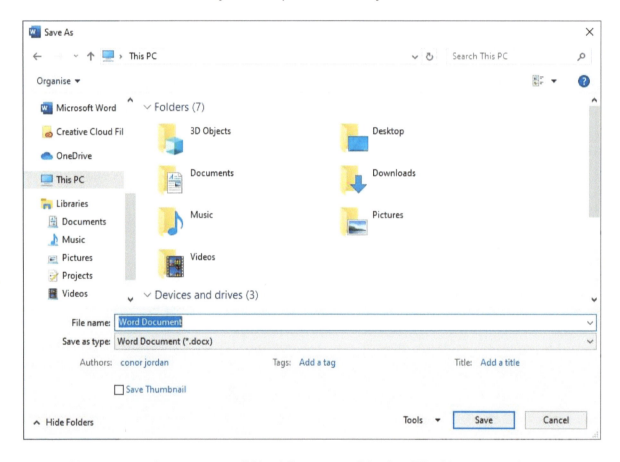

5. Name your document as "Word Document" in the **File Name** text box
6. Click **Save**

To Update/Overwrite a document, click on the **Save** icon on the left of the **Quick Access Toolbar**

Or use the keyboard shortcut **Ctrl+S** to save a document

To use this keyboard shortcut, hold down the **Ctrl** key and press the **S** key

Saving in Different Formats

You can save files in different formats so that they can be read by other applications such as older versions of Microsoft Word

You can save your document that can be read by any version of Microsoft Word in **Rich Text Format .rtf**

You can save your document as a **Plain Text .txt** file to save only text that can be read by all word processing software

1. With the "Word Document" file open, click on the **File Tab**
2. Choose **Save As** from the list of options
3. Click on the drop-down arrow from the **Save As Type** box
4. Choose **Rich Text Format (*.rtf)** to save your document in **Rich Text Format**
5. In the File name text box, call the file "CV"
6. Click on the **Save** button

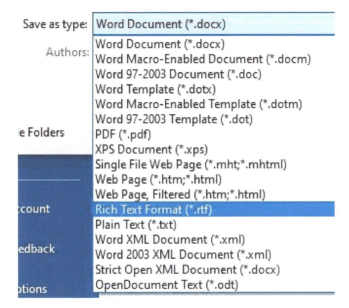

Plain Text Format

1. Click on the **File Tab**
2. Choose **Save As**
3. Click on the drop-down arrow from the **Save As Type** box
4. Choose **Plain Text (*.txt)** to save your document in **Plain Text Format**
5. In the File name text box, name the document "Plain"
6. Click on the **Save** button

Switch Between Documents

Create a new blank Word document while the current document is still open

With more than one document in **Word** open, hover over the **Word** icon in the taskbar and small preview windows for each open document appears

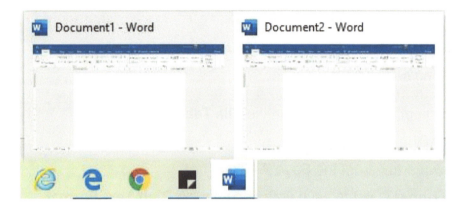

You can then click on **Document1** document to open that **Word** document

Switch back to **Document2**

Arrange All

On the **View** tab click the **Arrange All** button in the **Window** group and select the **Document1** document

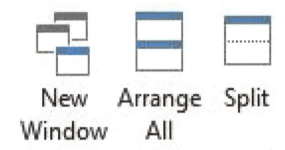

This will allow you to view both documents at the same time

Options

1. Click on the **File** tab

2. Select the **Options** button to view **Word Options**

3. To change where documents are saved, click on the **Save** button on the left hand-side of the dialog box

4. Select the **Browse** button beside the **Default Local File Location** text box

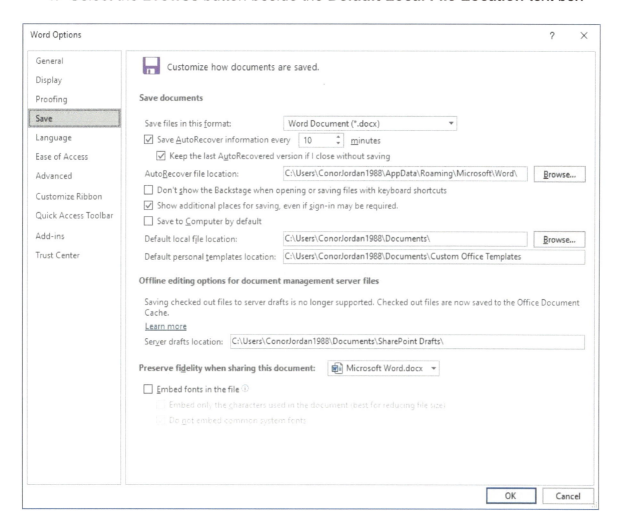

5. Choose a location on your computer to save documents

6. Click **OK**

7. Select **General** on the land hand-side of the dialog box

8. Enter in your **User Name** under **Personalize your copy of Microsoft Office**

9. Click **OK**

Help

Access the help facility to get help with common tasks in Word such as using the copy function or creating a table.

1. Click on the **Help Tab** in the centre of the **Ribbon**
2. Click on the **Help** button

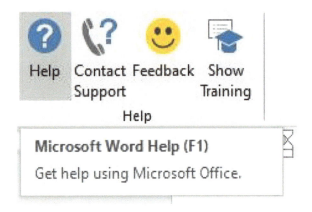

3. If connected to the internet, you can search for topics to help you use **Word**
4. You can browse **Popular Search** topics, use a **Get Started** option or type keywords into the **Search Box**

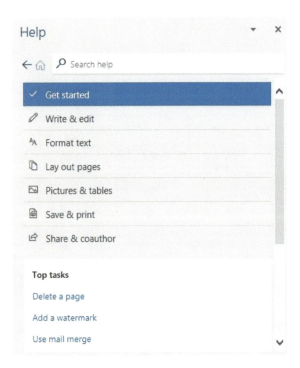

5. In the Search Box, type in "Create a Table" and press the **Enter** key

A list of helpful articles will appear providing you with information relating to creating a table

6. Click on one of the articles to find out more information about creating tables

Some articles have tutorial videos that can show you how to perform certain tasks

7. Click on the **Play** button to view the video
8. When you are finished, you can click on the **Home** icon to return to the main help page

Tell Me Box

Another way to access help in Microsoft Word is by using the **Tell Me** box

1. Type in "Chart" into the **Tell Me** box

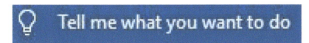

2. Select **Add a Chart** from the list of options that appear
3. Click **OK**

A chart will be inserted into the document

Zoom Control

There are magnification features in Microsoft Word that allow you to zoom in on text or graphics in a document. Using zoom tools allows you to choose how large or small text appears

You can increase and decrease the size of a document using the **Zoom Control** located on the bottom right of the window

1. Click and drag on the slider to increase or decrease the zoom
2. Alternatively, you can click on the minus or plus signs to increase or decrease the zoom

Setting Zoom

1. On the **View** tab in the **Zoom** group, select the **Zoom** button

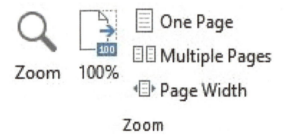

2. Set the zoom to 75%
3. Click OK

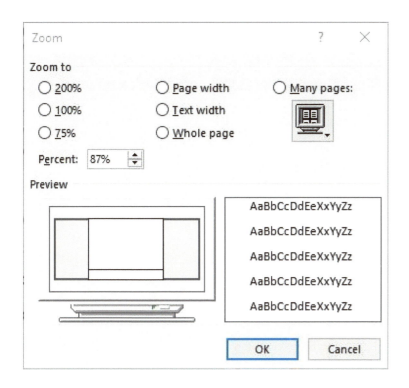

The document has been zoomed to a magnification of 75%

4. Click and drag the zoom slider at the bottom of the screen to readjust the zoom to 100%

Hide the Ribbon

1. On the right-hand side of the Ribbon next to the Editing group, click on

    Collapse the Ribbon

    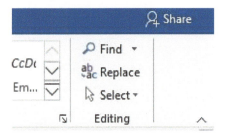

2. Click on **Ribbon Display Options**

3. Select Show **Tabs and Commands**

    This will show the ribbon again

Searching a Document

Find ▾
Replace
Select ▾

Editing

1. Open the document "Beyond the Gym"
2. On the **Home** tab in the **Editing** group select the **Find** button

The **Navigation** pane appears

3. Alternatively, you can use the **Ctrl+F** keyboard shortcut
4. Enter "energy" in the **Search Box** and press **Enter**

Each occurrence of that word will be highlighted in the document

5. You can cycle through every instance of the word using the **Up** and **Down** arrows below the search box
6. Click on the close button to hide the **Navigation** pane

Go To Tool

1. Open the "Healthy Diet" document

2. On the **Home** tab in the **Editing** group, select **Find**

3. Choose **Go To**

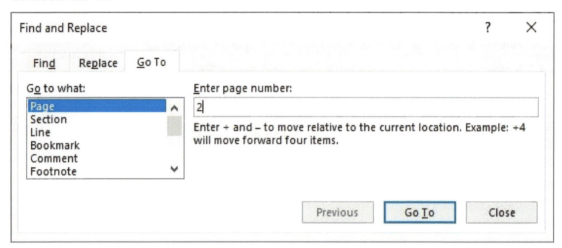

4. Under **Go To What**, select **Page**

5. In the **Enter Page Number** text box, enter "2"

6. Click on **Go To**

   Page 2 will be displayed

Revision Section 1

1. Open Microsoft Word
2. Create a Student Report from the templates available
3. Save the document as a Rich Text Format file called "Report"
4. Open another blank document
5. Switch back to the "Report" document and close it
6. Change where documents are saved to the Desktop
7. Return the original save location to Documents
8. Use the help facility to learn how to insert a picture
9. Use the Tell Me box to Insert a Chart
10. Change the Zoom to Page Width
11. Hide the Ribbon
12. Show the Ribbon again
13. Close the document without saving
14. Open the document "Festival"
15. Find every instance of "Festival" in the document
16. Use the Go To function to go to the second page
17. Close the document without saving

Section 2 – Document Creation

Views

Changing views in Microsoft Word allows you to see the content of your document in different ways

Depending on what type of document you are creating, selecting the most appropriate view will enable you to position text correctly, layout your document and design its content suitably

There are different views available in Word including **Draft, Outline, Read Mode, Web Layout** and **Print Layout**

Print Layout is the default view

1. Click on the **View Tab** and locate the **Views Group**

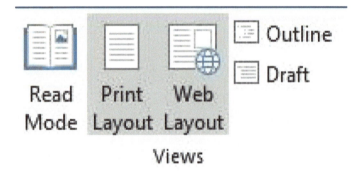

2. Click on the **Read Mode** to view your document in an easy to read view

This previews the document in the format you might see in an eReader app

3. Click on **Web Layout** to see the document as a web page

This can be used to view the document as it would appear as a web page

4. Click on **Outline** to view the document in this view

This displays headings and paragraphs as bullet points that can be changed according to the user's requirements

5. Select **Close Outline View** to return to **Print Layout** view
6. Click on **Draft** to see a draft of your Word document

Entering text into a document

1. Type in the following text:

"There is no doubt that getting up off the couch is better for you than lazing around. But you do need a change of scenery and something exciting and challenging to stimulate yourself. By getting out in the fresh air and getting involved in group activities such as fitness classes, yoga or spinning classes, you greatly improve your physical health and create a huge impact upon your mental well-being."

2. Type in your name after the paragraph
3. On the **Insert Tab** click the **Symbol** button in the **Symbol** group

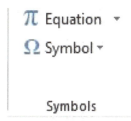

A drop-down menu will appear

4. Choose **More Symbols** from the list of available options

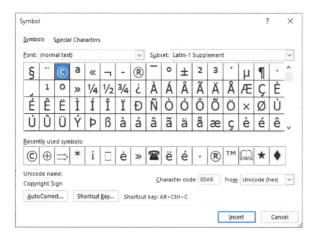

5. Click on the **Font Drop-Down Box**
6. Scroll down and select the **Adobe Caslon Pro** font
7. Choose a symbol to place in your document such as the **Copyright Symbol** ©
8. Save the document as "Exercise"

Show/Hide Characters

The **Show/Hide** function allows characters that will not be printed to be viewed on screen. Characters such as tabs, spaces and paragraph marks can be shown or hidden using this button.

This button is located on the right-hand side of the **Paragraph** group

Enter is shown by a **Paragraph Mark:** ¶

Press the **Enter** key and notice the appearance of this mark

A **Tab** is shown by this mark: →

Create a **Tab** paragraph mark by pressing the **Tab** key

Spaces are shown by dots: ············

Press the **Spacebar** key to create spaces characterised by dots

Line Breaks

You use **Line Breaks** when you want text to appear on two lines but to be treated as if it were a single line. The character looks like this: ↵

After a line of text, hold down the **Shift** key and press **Enter**

Page Breaks

This is used to start a new page

On the **Insert** tab, in the **Pages** group select **Page Break** or press **Ctrl+Enter**

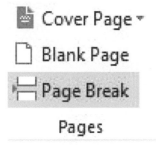

Pages

Place the cursor after a **Page Break** and press the **Backspace** key to remove it

Editing Text

Users can edit and manipulate text in Word by selecting, typing, editing and deleting. There are a range of methods that can be used to change how text is structured in a document.

Selecting Text

1. Open the document "Online Shopping"
2. Left click and drag over the first word "Online" to select it
3. Start typing "Digital"
4. The word has been replaced

There are other ways to select text

1. Double click on the word "retailers" in the first paragraph to select it
2. Press the **Delete** key
3. Type in "shops"

Selecting a sentence

1. You can select a sentence by holding down the **Ctrl** key and clicking once inside of it
2. Try this method by clicking inside the first sentence

The Selection Bar

The **Selection Bar** is the empty space on the left-hand side of the page used to select text. You can use this to highlight a range of text in a document.

1. Move the mouse to the left-hand side of the page until the mouse pointer changes direction
2. Click once to select the first line of text beginning with "Online shopping"

There are other ways of using the selection bar

1. Double click to select the first paragraph
2. You can then type over this to create a new first paragraph

Selecting an Entire Document

1. Treble click on the **Selection Bar** to select an entire document
2. Alternatively, you can use the keyboard shortcut **Ctrl+A**

You can also click and drag on the **Selection Bar** to highlight text

Replace

The **Replace** function allows you to replace specific words in a document

1. On the **Home** tab in the **Editing** group select **Replace**

2. In the **Find What** text box, enter "shopping"
3. In the **Replace With** text box, enter "buying"
4. Select the **Replace** button to replace one instance of the word
5. Select the **Replace All** button to replace every instance of the word in the document
6. Save the document as "Online Shopping"

Copy, Paste and Cut

These commands allow you to move text around a document

Copy copies text to the **Clipboard**, **Cut** removes the text from the document and copies it to the **Clipboard** and **Paste** places the text in a new location in the document

1. Open the document "Our Natural Resource"
2. Highlight the sentence beginning "Throughout history…"
3. Select **Copy** from the **Clipboard** group

4. Place the **Insertion Point** after "…down the drain"
5. Select Paste from the Clipboard group

   The first sentence has now been copied to the end of the first paragraph

6. Highlight the second sentence beginning "The earliest of…"
7. Select **Cut** from the **Clipboard** group
8. Place the **Insertion Point** after "…for human consumption."
9. Select **Paste** from the **Clipboard** group
10. The text has been moved
11. Open a new document
12. Copy the first paragraph beginning "Throughout history…" with the keyboard shortcut **Ctrl+C**
13. Use the taskbar to switch to the new document
14. Use the keyboard shortcut **Ctrl+V**

    The paragraph is pasted into a new document

15. Save the document as "Copied"

Revision Section 2

1. Open the document "CV"
2. Fill in your own information under Personal Details
3. Insert a Telephone symbol before your telephone number
4. Show all Paragraph Marks in the document
5. Insert a Line Break after the Curriculum Vitae title
6. Insert a Page Break after the Employment section
7. Edit the first row in the Education table to include your own details
8. Select the entire document using the Selection Bar
9. Replace every instance of "Job" with "Employment"
10. Copy the Employment section to appear at the end of the document
11. Cut and Paste the Education section to appear after the Employment section
12. Save the document as "My CV"

Section 3 – Formatting

Font

A font is a style of text such as `Courier New` or Times New Roman

There are a wide range of font styles that can be applied to text

1. Open the document "A Man's Best Friend"
2. Highlight the first paragraph beginning "The elderly man…"
3. On the **Home** tab in the **Font** group, click on the drop-down arrow

4. Select the Segoe UI font
5. Highlight the heading "A Man's Best Friend"
6. To the right of the **Font** box, click on the drop-down arrow next to the number to choose a **Font Size**
7. Change the font size to 16
8. Save the document as "Font"

Bold, Italic and Underline

1. Open the document "A Summer Day"

2. Highlight the heading "A Summer Day"

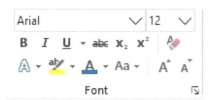

3. In the **Font** group on the **Home** tab, locate the **Bold** button to make text **Bold**

4. Or use the keyboard shortcut **Ctrl+B**

5. Highlight the first sentence beginning "All three of us…"

6. Click on the **Italic** button to make text *Italic* or press **Ctrl+I**

7. Highlight the heading "A Summer Day" again

8. Click on the **Underline** button to <u>Underline</u> words or press **Ctrl+U**

Subscript and Superscript

Subscript makes the text lower than other text

Superscript makes the text higher than other

1. Open a new document and type the following text:

    "The chemical name for water is H20

    The chemical name for air is 02"

2. Highlight the 2 after H
3. In the Font group, click on the **Subscript** button to make it lower than the other text

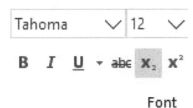

Font

4. Highlight the 2 after the O
5. Click on the **Superscript** button in the Font group to make it higher than the other text

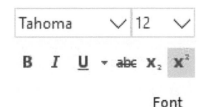

Font

Font Colour

1. Open the document "On the Run"

2. Highlight the first paragraph beginning "Wind rushing…"

3. Click on the **Font Colour** arrow beside the button on the right of the **Font** group

4. Select a green colour from **Standard Colors**

5. Highlight the second paragraph beginning "Her ponytail…"

6. Select a light blue colour from **Theme Colors**

Altering Case

Sentence case is where the first letter of a sentence is uppercase

lowercase is where all letters are in small case

UPPERCASE is where all letters are capitalised

Capitalise Each Word is where all words begin with an uppercase letter

tOGGLE cASE converts every character to the opposite of what it is

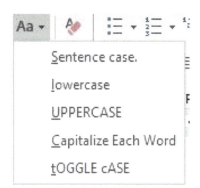

1. Open the document "Early Morning"
2. Highlight the heading
3. In the Font group select Change Case
4. Change it to UPPERCASE
5. Highlight the first sentence
6. Change it to lowercase
7. Highlight the second sentence beginning "Every sinew…"
8. Change it to Capitalize Each Word

Hyphenation

Hyphens split words onto two lines to make use of space in a document.

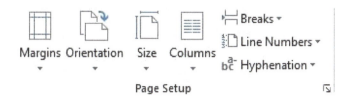

1. Open the document "Check Up"

2. Select the **Hyphenation** button on the **Page Setup** group on the **Layout** tab and select **Automatic.** This applies hyphenation to the document

3. Select **Manual** to manually check each occurrence of hyphenation in the document

4. Save the document as "Hyphenation"

Hyperlinks

Hyperlinks allow you to link a word, sentence or picture to another part of the document, another document or a website

1. Open the document "Hyperlinks"
2. Highlight the heading "Writing"
3. On the **Insert** tab in the **Links** group select **Links**

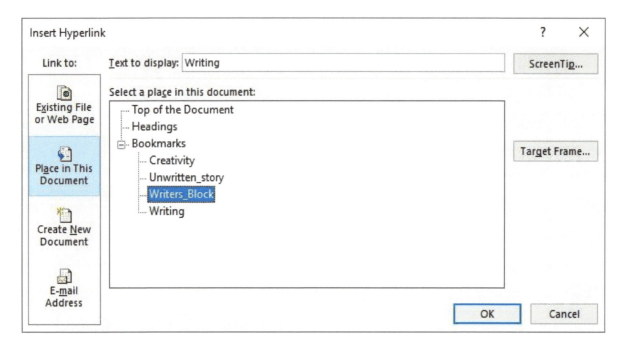

4. Select **Place in This Document**
5. Under **Bookmarks** choose **Writers_Block**
6. Click **OK**
7. Return to the first page
8. Hold down the **Ctrl** key and click on the **Writing** heading
9. The hyperlink will bring you to the second page
10. Scroll to the end of the document
11. Type www.icdl.org
12. Highlight the address
13. On the **Insert** tab in the **Links** group, select **Link**

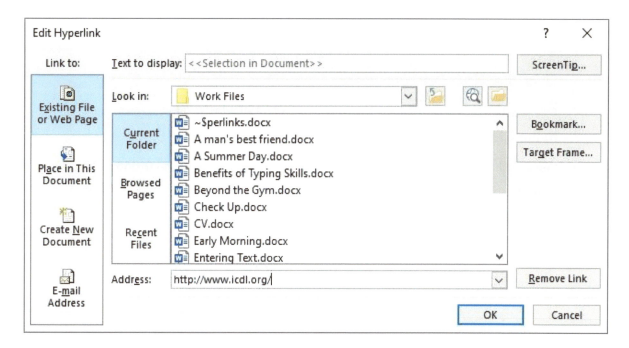

14. Type http://www.icdl.org into the **Address** text box

15. Click **OK**

16. Hold down the **Ctrl** key and click on the link

17. If connected to the internet you will be brought to that website

18. Right-click on the ICDL address

19. Select **Remove Link**

20. The link has been removed

Merging Paragraphs

1. Open the "New Year" document

2. Highlight the first paragraph beginning "With the New Year…"

3. In the **Clipboard** group, select **Copy**

4. After the end of the paragraph ending "…a healthy weight" press the **Enter** key

5. Click on the **Paste** drop-down arrow

6. Choose **Merge Formatting**

7. The formatting of the first and second paragraphs will be merged

Line Breaks

You use **Line Breaks** when you want text to appear on two lines but to be treated as if it were a single line. They are also called **Soft Carriage Returns**

1. Open the "Keeping Fit" document
2. At the beginning of the document type "Keeping Fit"
3. Place the insertion point after "Keeping"
4. Hold down the **Shift** key and press **Enter**
5. The heading will be treated as a single line but appear on two lines

Alignment

You can align text to the Left, Center, Right or you can Justify your text which makes the text have straight left and right-hand margins

1. Open the "Technology" document
2. Highlight the first paragraph beginning "The global village…"
3. On the **Home** tab in the **Paragraph** group select this button to align selected text to the **Left**

4. Highlight the second paragraph and **Center** align selected text with this button:

5. Highlight the third paragraph and align selected text to the **Right** with this button:

6. Highlight the fourth paragraph and **Justify** text using this button:

Indenting Paragraphs

Indents move the text further to the right than other paragraphs

1. Open the document "Festival"
2. Place the cursor to the left of the first paragraph
3. Press the **Tab** key to indent the first line of the paragraph
4. Place the cursor to the left of the second paragraph
5. Click on the **Increase Indent** button in the **Paragraph** group to indent the paragraph

6. Place the cursor to the left of the second paragraph
7. Click on the **Decrease Indent** button in the **Paragraph** group to remove the indent

8. Click on the **View** tab in the **Show** group select **Ruler** to show the **Ruler** at the top of the document

☑ Ruler

☐ Gridlines

☐ Navigation Pane

    Show

9. Click on the **Paragraph Dialog Box Launcher**

10. Change the **Left** and **Right Indentation** to 1cm

11. Adjust the **Special Indentation** to **Hanging**

12. Click **OK**

You can also click and drag the top arrow on the ruler to change the position of the indent

Tab Settings

Tabs align vertical rows of text in a document. Adjust the tab settings to change the layout of a document so that the document appears presentable.

1. Open the document "Tabs"
2. Show the **Ruler** and click on the **Paragraph Dialog Box Launcher** on the **Home** tab
3. Click the **Tabs** button

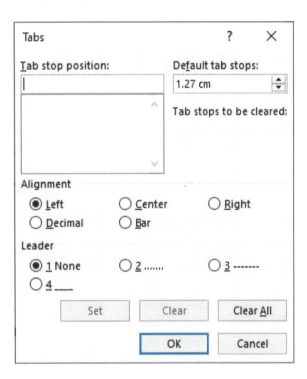

4. Enter 2cm in the **Tab Stop Position** box
5. Set the **Alignment** as **Left** to apply left alignment to the tab
6. Set the **Leader** as **None**
7. Click **Set** then **OK**
8. Or left click just beneath the ruler to set a tab

Tab Alignment

1. Set two tab positions on the **Ruler** at 6cm and 10cm and double-click the tab position at 6cm
2. Select the **Right** option from the **Alignment** selections and click **Set**
3. Select the 10cm tab position and make it **Center** aligned and click **Set**
4. Click **OK**

This will vertically align text typed into your document at the specified positions

5. Save the document as "Layout"

Paragraph Spacing

When applying paragraph spacing it is good practice to include spacing between paragraphs rather than inserting several paragraph marks.

1. Open the document "Journey"
2. Highlight all of the text in the document
3. Click on the **Paragraph** group dialog box launcher

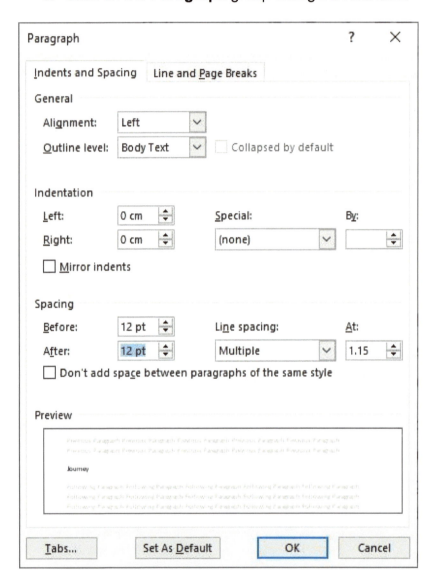

4. Under **Spacing** apply a 12 pt spacing **Before** and **After** each paragraph
5. Under Line Spacing select 1.5
6. Click **OK**

Notice the effect it has on the document

Word

Bullets and Numbering

Bullets and numbering can be applied to a list. Style of bullets and numbering can be changed to suit the document's design and purpose.

1. Open the document "Shopping List"
2. Highlight the first list of items
3. In the **Paragraph** group select **Bullets**

   Notice the effect this has had on the list

4. Select the **Bullets** button again to remove the bullets from the list
5. Click on the arrow to the right of the **Bullets** button

Recently Used Bullets

Bullet Library

Document Bullets

6. Choose a **Bullets** style

This will be applied to the list

7. Scroll down the document and highlight the second list of items
8. In the **Paragraph** group select **Numbering**

The items in the list will be numbered

9. Click on the arrow beside the Numbering button
10. Select the Numbering Alignment Left 1) 2) 3) option
11. This numbering style is applied to the list
12. Save the document

Borders and Shading

Borders can be applied to paragraphs using a variety of different styles. Shading in a range of different colours can be applied to paragraphs in a document.

1. Open the "Festival" document
2. Highlight the first paragraph beginning "I know most festival…"
3. Click on the arrow beside the **Borders** button in the **Paragraph** group
4. Choose **Borders and Shading**

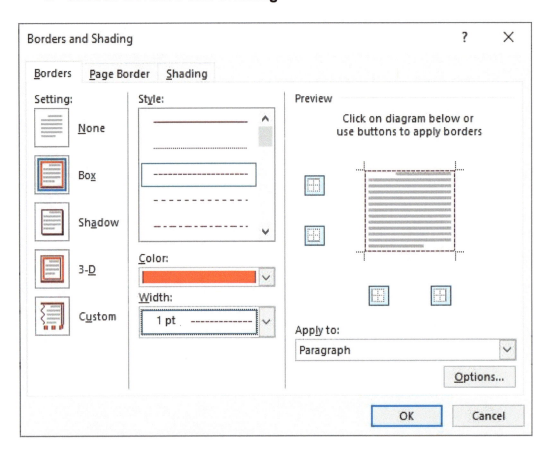

5. Under **Setting** choose **Box**
6. Choose a **Dashed Line** style for the border
7. Select a **Red** colour
8. Change the border **Width** to 1pt
9. Click on the **Shading** tab
10. For **Color**, choose Blue Accent 1 Lighter 60%
11. Click **OK**
12. Save the document as Borders

Character and Paragraph Styles

Word has a selection of styles that can be applied to headings and paragraphs in a document.

1. Open the "A Summer Day" document
2. Highlight the heading
3. In the **Styles** group click on the **Style** dialog box launcher

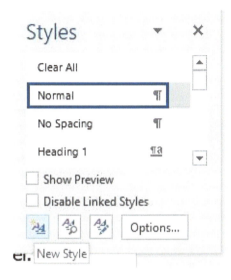

4. Select the **New Style** button

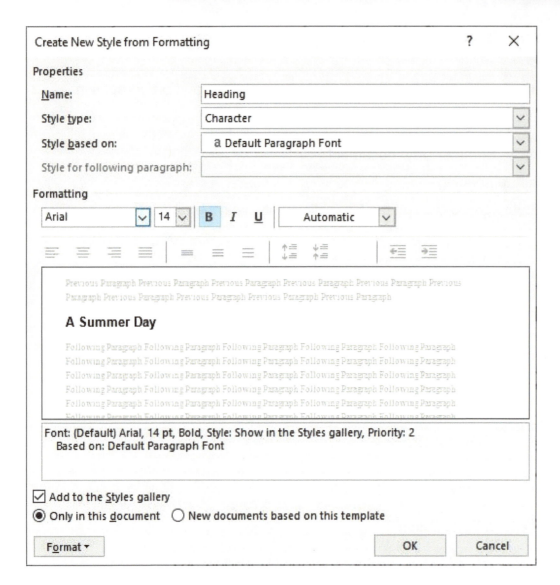

5. Enter the name "Heading" and the **Style Type** as **Character**

6. Change the **Formatting** to Arial, 14 pt, Bold

7. Click **OK**

8. Highlight the first paragraph in the document

9. In the **Styles** group select the dialog box launcher and choose **New Style**

10. Enter the name "Paragraph" and the **Style Type** as **Paragraph**

11. Format the text as Arial, 12 pt and apply Italics

12. Click **OK**

13. Save the document as "Styles"

Copy Format Tool

The Format Painter allows you to copy the formatting applied to a paragraph to another paragraph

1. Open the document "Format Painter"
2. Select the first paragraph
3. On the **Home** tab in the **Clipboard** group, select **Format Painter**

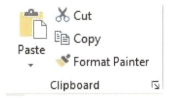

4. Highlight the second paragraph

The formatting will be applied to the second paragraph

Revision Section 3

1. Open the document "Keeping Fit"
2. Change the Font to Arial, size 14
3. Make the heading "Fitness Centres" Bold and Underlined
4. Apply Italics to the paragraphs
5. Type another heading at the end saying "Stay Hydrated with H2O"
6. Apply Superscript to the number 2
7. Change the heading font colours to Green
8. Make the headings all Uppercase
9. Apply Automatic Hyphenation to the document
10. Insert a Hyperlink with the document "Beyond the Gym"
11. Merge the Formatting between the headings and the paragraphs
12. Centre Align all headings
13. Apply a Hanging indent to the first paragraph
14. Align both paragraphs with Tabs to 2cm
15. Apply a paragraph spacing of 6 pt Before and After each paragraph with a 1.5 line spacing
16. Number each heading
17. Apply a blue border with a light-yellow shaded background to the first paragraph
18. Apply a consistent Style of a Veranda font, 16 pt, Bold to every heading
19. Use the Format Painter to apply the new heading style to the paragraphs
20. Save the document as "Fitness"

Section 4 – Tables

Tables can be used to store information in an easy to read format. You can choose the number of columns and rows to be used in the table as well as its design and layout.

1. Open a new blank document
2. On the **Insert** tab in the **Tables** group, select **Table**

3. Enter in 6 for the **Number of Columns** and 3 for the **Number of Rows**
4. Click **OK**
5. Click on the symbol on the top left-hand side of the table
6. Press the **Backspace** key

The table is deleted

7. Select the **Undo** button on the **Quick Access Toolbar**
8. Enter in the following information into the table:

	Monday	Tuesday	Wednesday	Thursday	Friday
Week 1	4 miles	3 miles	5 miles	Rest Day	2 miles
Week 2	5 miles	4 miles	3 miles	Rest Day	2 miles

9. Change the days of the week to abbreviations e.g. Mon., Tues., Wed.
10. Save the document as "Training Plan"

Editing Tables

1. With the "Training Plan" document still open hover your mouse over the bottom left of the table
2. Click on the plus sign to insert a new row
3. Type in the following information:

Week 3	6 miles	4 miles	2 miles	Rest Day	7 miles

4. Change Wednesday on Week 1 to 4 miles and Friday Week 2 to 3 miles
5. Hover the cursor over the left-hand side of the first row
6. Make the text bold
7. Hover the cursor over the Monday column and change the formatting to Underline
8. Hover the cursor between the first and second row
9. Click and drag to make the row height increase
10. Highlight the Week 3 row and press Backspace to delete that row
11. Save the document

Table Formatting

A variety of styles can be applied to tables to make their appearance more distinctive and attractive.

1. Open the "Training Plan" document
2. Select the entire table
3. On the **Table Tools – Layout** tab in the **Cell Size** group, adjust the **Height** to 1cm and the **Width** to 2.5 cm

4. On the **Table Tools – Design** tab in the **Borders** group select **Borders** and choose **Borders and Shading**

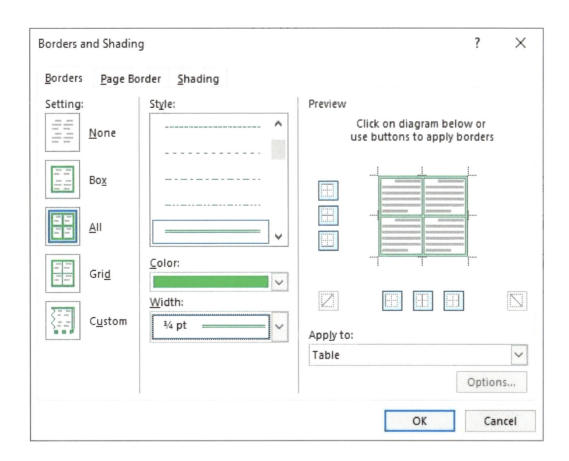

5. Change the line **Style** to **Double** and **Color** to Green

6. Change the line **Width** to ¾ pt

7. Click **OK**

8. Click on the **Shading** tab

9. Apply a **Fill Color** of Orange Accent 2 Lighter 60%

10. Click **OK**

The format of the table has been changed

Objects

1. Open a new document

2. On the **Insert** tab in the **Text** group select **Object**

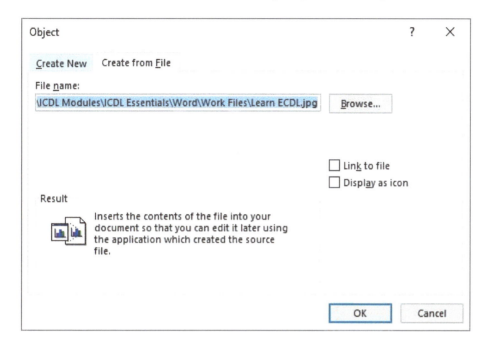

3. Select the **Create From File** tab

4. Click **Browse** and navigate to the **Work Files** folder

5. Select the Learn ECDL image

6. Click **OK**

7. Click **OK** again

8. The image is inserted into the document

9. Click on the image to select it

10. Open a new document

11. On the **Home** tab in the **Clipboard** group, select **Copy**

12. Make the new document active

13. Place your cursor in the new document

14. On the **Home** tab in the **Clipboard** group, select **Paste**

15. Hover the cursor over the bottom right hand corner of the image

16. Click and drag to resize the image

17. If you want to maintain image proportions, hold down the **Shift** key while resizing

18. Press the **Backspace** key to delete the picture and close the document

Revision Section 4

1. Open a new document
2. Insert a table with six columns and three rows
3. Enter in the following information:

Walking Routine

	Monday	Tuesday	Wednesday	Thursday	Friday
Week 1	20 mins	35 mins	45 mins	25 mins	Rest Day
Week 2	25 mins	40 mins	50 mins	30 mins	Rest Day

4. Select the entire table
5. Change the Cell Height to 1.5cm
6. Apply a blue double line border to the table
7. Beneath the table, insert the image file "Trail.jpg"
8. Resize the image to a suitable size while maintaining its proportions
9. Save the document as "Walking Plan"

Section 5 – Mail Merge

Mail Merge is used to combine a **Data Source** with a **Main Document**. It is often used for mailing lists or sending out the same letter addressed to different people.

The **Data Source** contains a table of information that will be used for the **Mail Merge** usually with address details.

First you create the **Main Document**. This could be a letter, e-mail messages, envelops or labels.

1. Open a blank document
2. On the **Mailings** tab select the **Start Mail Merge** button
3. Select the **Step by Step Mail Merge Wizard** to display the **Mail Merge** task pane on the right-hand side of the screen

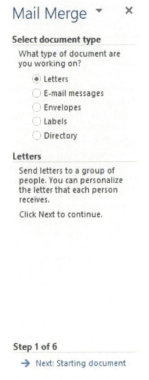

4. Select **Letters** from the **Select Document Type** list
5. Click **Next: Starting Document** to proceed to step two

Step 1 of 6

→ Next: Starting document

6. At step two choose to **Use the Current Document**

7. Select the **Next: Select Recipients** button

Step 2 of 6

→ Next: Select recipients

Using a Data Source

Make sure you are on **Step 3: Select Recipients** of the **Step-by-Step Mail Merge Wizard**

1. Select **Use an Existing List** under Select Recipients
2. Select **Browse** under **Use an Existing List**
3. Locate the **Address List** file in the **Work Files** folder
4. Click **OK**

Writing your Letter

1. Click on **Next: Write Your Letter**
2. Type the following letter:

Dear

I am writing to you regarding a special offer we are giving loyal customers who have been with the company for over a year.

I am delighted to inform you that you will receive a 25% discount on all laptops and tablets in store. The discount is valid until the end of this month.

Regards

Harry Smith

Store Manager

3. Create space at the top of the document
4. Place the cursor at the start of the document
5. On the **Mailings** tab in the **Write & Insert Fields** group, select **Insert Merge Fields**
6. Insert the following merge fields:

«First_Name»

«Last_Name»

«Address_Line_1»

«Address_Line_2»

«Town»

Dear «Title» «Last_Name»

7. On the **Mailings** tab click on **Finish & Merge**

8. Choose **Edit Individual Documents**

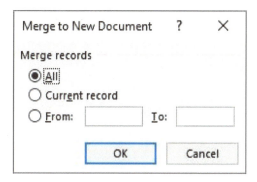

9. Click **OK**

10. Preview the merged letters

11. Save the document as "Discount"

12. On the **File** tab select **Print**

13. Select the **Print** button

Revision Section 5

1. Open the "Fast Car Services" document
2. Begin a Mail Merge using the existing data source "Customer List"
3. Insert the following merge fields:

«First_Name»

«Last_Name»

«Address_Line_1»

«Address_Line_2»

«City»

Dear «Title» «First_Name» «Last_Name»

4. Complete the merge
5. Preview your letters
6. Print all of your letters

Section 6 – Document Setup

1. Open the "Day Trip" document

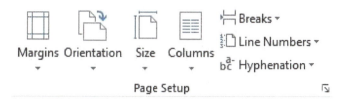

2. On the **Layout** tab in the **Page Setup** group, select **Orientation**
3. Change the orientation to **Landscape**
4. Select **Size**
5. Choose **Letter**
6. Select Margins and choose Custom Margins

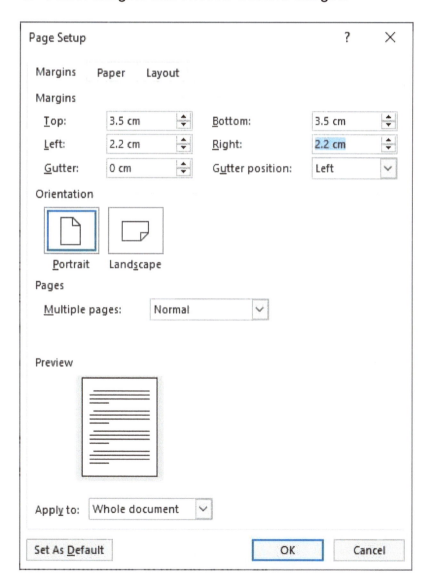

7. Change the **Top** and **Bottom** margins to 3.5cm and the **Left** and Right margins to 2.2cm

8. Click **OK**

9. Place the cursor after the first paragraph

10. On the **Layout** tab in the **Page Setup** group, select **Breaks**

11. Choose **Page Break**

12. Press the Backspace key twice to remove the page break

13. Save the document

Headers & Footers

Headers contain information that appears at the top of each page. They can contain page numbers, dates, author's name among other details. Footers appear at the bottom of each page and can be used for a range of different pieces of information.

1. Open the "Day Trip" document
2. On the **Insert** tab in the **Header & Footer** group select **Header**
3. Select **Edit Header**
4. Type your name into the **Header**
5. Press the **Tab** key twice
6. On the **Header & Footer Tools – Design** tab in the **Insert** group, select **Date & Time**

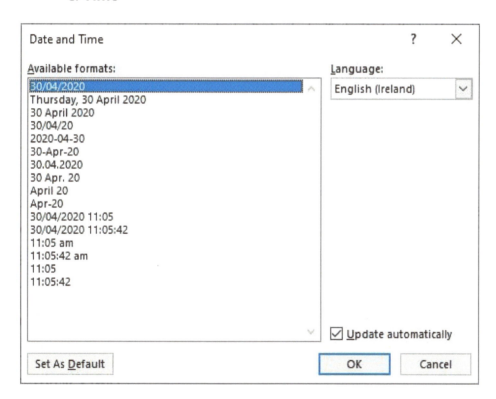

7. Choose the first date format and click OK
8. In the **Navigation** group, select **Go To Footer**
9. Select **Page Number** and choose **Bottom of Page**
10. Choose **Plain Number 1**
11. Press the **Tab** key twice
12. In the **Insert** group select **Document Info**
13. Choose **File Name**

14. Choose **Close Header and Footer**

15. Save and close "Day Trip"

Spell Check

Word allows you to review a document by checking spelling and grammar. You can cycle through each misspelt word and decide to accept or reject the suggested change. You also have the option to add a new word to the dictionary if Word does not currently have it stored.

1. Open the document "Love Letter"
2. On the **Review** tab select **Spelling & Grammar**

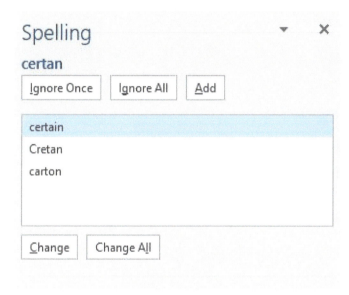

3. Click on the **Change** button to accept the spelling suggestion
4. For the "down" spelling, select the correct spelling from the list of suggestions provided
5. Choose to **Delete** the repeated "our" word
6. Add the name "O'Mahony" to the dictionary so that Word will use this word in future
7. Ignore the suggested punctuation change after the word "weary"
8. Continue to accept the suggested spelling changes throughout the document
9. Save the document as "Checked"

Print a Document

1. Open the document "A Walk Through Town"

2. Highlight the first paragraph

3. On the **File** tab select **Print**

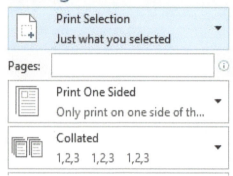

4. Under **Settings** choose **Print Selection**

5. This will only print the first paragraph

6. Change the **Settings** again to **Print All Pages**

7. After **Pages**, enter 2

8. This will only print page 2

9. Beside the **Print** button, change the number of copies to 3

10. Click **Print**

11. Three copies of the second page of the document will be printed

Revision Section 6

1. Open the document "Technology"
2. Change the orientation to Landscape
3. Adjust the size to Letter
4. Change all Margins to 3cm
5. Insert a Page Break after the second paragraph
6. Insert a Header with your name and the Date on the right of the header
7. Insert the File Name in the Footer
8. Spell Check the document for errors
9. Print preview the document
10. Print only the first two paragraphs

www.ingramcontent.com/pod-product-compliance
Lightning Source LLC
LaVergne TN
LVHW060201050326
832903LV00016B/339